SOUL MURDER
Attachment Traumas and Social Hypnotism

KAREN KELLOCK PH.D.

Manual for
Superior Men

A complete theory based on Einstein physics,
Political Psychology, Systems Theory
and Archetypal Psychiatry.

FORMULA
All success attraction
All disease obstruction
All recovery elimination

You must fast on all three
OBSTRUCTIONS:
People
Habit
Food

SOUL MURDER

The more public her smear campaign the happier she is: the more humiliating, the better her image. How it shocks when someone you admired is de-pedestalized and shown to be a dam liar. Narcissists will do anything to win--any sabotaging, cruel thing: that's why to cut the chain. Learn about narcissists, for it protects. Spirituality brings the life and peace of God but soul ties are a stronghold keeping bad in/good out. Shifting life in a spiritual direction is the only way to get out of a soul tie relationship of destruction.

SOUL MURDER
Attachment Traumas and Social Hypnotism

LOW SELF-ESTEEM IS IN OUR DNA
THEY BLOVIATE ON CELL PHONES
THE VALUE OF GOOD TEAMWORK
GRUESOME TWOSOMES
RUDENESS GET THE HELL OUT
SYSTEM CHANGES SUDDENLY
THE ERA OF SOCIAL NARCISSISTS
HE CALLS HIMSELF A "PLAYER"
BREAK TIES TO TOXIC PEOPLE
CARNIVORE EXPERIMENT: YUK!
FIRST REACTION TO POISON IS GOOD
SUDDEN INTEREST IN NARCISSISM
BROUGHT UP IN A TINY CABIN
DIETARY [HORMONAL] CHANGES ON MOOD
THRU JESUS A FRESH START
TV AND THE OCCULT
TRUE APOSTLES WERE DESTITUTE
ENEMIES OF THE CROSS
FEELING IMPOSED ON
NEED A LOCKED GATE
TRIGGERED INVESTIGATIVE BEHAVIORS
WORKS DOCTRINES FAIL
WORKERS ARE BEWITCHED
STOP DICTATING
HOMILECTICS: ART OF PREACHING
FAKES ARE ARROGANT AND MEAN
CHURCHES AND LEADERS BEWITCHED
QUESTION INTENSE ATTRACTIONS
BE SWEPT UP BY GOD NOT MAN
WICKED MEN WORMING THEIR WAY IN
SEEING YOURSELF AS WORTHELSS
TRAUMA THE SOUL BINDER
FIND AREA, ASK GOD TO CLEAN IT OUT
AVOID ALLEY CATS
R. BIG IS A PUNY LITTLE MAN
ASK GOD TO REMOVE IT ALL, EVEN SOCIAL

SOUL MURDER
Attachment Traumas and Social Hypnotism

HE BROUGHT YOU UNDER
MARRYING EX-ALLEY CATS
DEFINE YOURSELF OR SOMEONE WILL
A QUEEN FUNCTIONING AS A SLAVE
OBSESSIVE UNREQUITED LOVE
LOVE CRUTCHES AND ADDICTIONS
DO YOUR WORK NOW ATTRACT THE ONE
BE IN CONTROL OF YOUR SOUL
MIRTH/PARTYING FOLLOWED BY SORROW
MATURITY IS SELF-AWARENESS
LIKE MOM SAID LIFE'S A BITCH
IF YOU'RE SMART THEY HATE YOU
THE PROBLEM IS ALWAYS PEOPLE
SYSTEMS OF DYSFUNCTION LAST
THEY SIZE YOU UP & GOSSIP
SPIRALING DOWN PROCESS
ENDGAME THOUGHTS
PROSPERITY AND RESTORED YOUTH
MIXED SIGNALS FROM FRENEMIES
NO EMPATHY/PATHOLOGICAL ENVY
NARC FEMALES ALWAYS ENVY, *ALWAYS*
IF YOU KNOW A WOMAN LIKE THIS
THEY HATE YOU SUDDENLY
LIBERALISM AND NARCISSISM
VIRTUE SIGNALING IS NOT MORALITY
SHE GOSSIPS FOR CONTROL
BECAUSE YOU GET NO MEANING
INCONSISTENT REINFORCEMENT
THEY HATE YOUR BOUNDARIES
MAKING FUN OF YOUR NEEDS
NARCISSISTIC INJURY/PUSHBACKS
IT TAKES A LIFE TO REALIZE
FROM ABUSE TO BEAUTIFUL VIEWS
DRIP DRIP DRIP DEVALUATION
PEOPLE LOVERS OR VIRTUE SIGNALERS?
BE EXCLUSIVE, NOT INCLUSIVE

SOUL MURDER

Attachment Traumas and Social Hypnotism

SOUL MURDER

LOW SELF-ESTEEM IS IN OUR DNA

Low self-esteem is in our DNA as women and no one's a queen but it's a perfect model we think.

Love Bombing, intimacy avoidance, gaslighting, breadcrumbing--who needs these things?

Stop resenting those past actors too. It shows extreme ingratitude after God rescued you.

Shifting life in a spiritual direction is the only way to get out of a soul tie relationship of destruction.

Spirituality brings the life and peace of God. Soul ties are a stronghold keeping bad in/good out.

The stronghold contradicts everything you know about the mind of God like debauchery and fraud.

You must discern what level the tie is on. Why is this bond so strong? Only God reveals this son.

THEY BLOVIATE ON CELL PHONES

I hate phones cuz people bloviate and you gotta listen to it. Emails are perfect cuz you choose it.

How it shocks when someone you admired is depedestalized and shown to be a dam liar.

How it hurts, how it has hurt! How to get free of a soul tie relationship with an abusive jerk?

SOUL MURDER

God has His own timetable and only He knows it so stop saying I should put deadlines on myself.

Deadlines are hazardous if you live in the right brain of timeless space--don't do this to me ok.

How I got away: he gave me incredibly bad advice, he was depedestalized and I was finally free.

The soul tie had me bound, a stronghold wouldn't let me out. There's always escape if you ask God.

THE VALUE OF GOOD TEAMWORK

I finally saw the value of teamwork, she lived in the guest cottage and together we came first.

Once I saw that I fixed the cottage up real nice cuz now we're a team and this helps the enterprise.

Time [and this] will pass, you'll remember it no more but those lessons you'll never forget of import.

Tho' she was trapped in mental illness she still saw what was happening and their disrespecting.

She couldn't escape her illness but saw the treachery as they took control without conscience.

The movie Gaslight showed how mental illness is created by another--collapse with trauma.

While being held under God promised one day I'd tell all about this group tyranny and soul murder.

The movie Gaslight showed how mental illness is created by another & collapse with trauma.

GRUESOME TWOSOMES

SOUL MURDER

Folie a deux, gruesome twosomes, sick systems: it's all about games of folly bigger than the person.

The recovered insane recall how he was treated when down and their reactions to him grown.

He was trapped, controlled and unable to defend himself. In a panic for survival, all due to gossip.

Stupid, silly & shallow--that's all I got from you gal. Either grow up or leave me alone for awhile.

If you wanna be famous you gotta put up with this: mischaracterizations of a who you are sis.

RUDENESS GET THE HELL OUT

If you're gonna be rude to me out you go. I'm done putting up with coarse and gross folk.

To be a success cut all ties to the herd. Hang with people like you and success is assured.

When they saw me as a grasshopper I was floored and so unprepared I even thought it of myself.

The more tied to family the more false projections act as a script which you act out willingly.

When they saw me as a grasshopper I was so floored and unprepared I saw myself as inferior.

It's the system relationships which defines us. I am up cuz you're down: a purely relational matrix.

I had to escape these constant comparisons and just be me again. I was nuts while in that system.

SYSTEM CHANGES SUDDENLY

SOUL MURDER

You're high as a kite then sister drags your identity through the mud and weak you take it on.

His horribly bad advice broke the stronghold of nothing getting in/nothing changing and I got bold.

It's a trickle to heaven and a flood to hell. Remember that when learning to discern two worlds.

Perceptive or paranoid? Often reading between the lines/seeing hidden meanings God anoints.

I never saw since fake charlatans in my life. Standing stiffnecked acting so arrogant as if right.

THE ERA OF SOCIAL NARCISSISTS

Those people are so impressed with themselves--a whole generation of fools and tramps.

If you're sickened by a person that's it: recognize it and don't cover it over with liberal narratives.

Take his bad advice as a ticket outa hell and the destructions/pain of being under his spell.

If a bad relationship God has an escape for you. Look carefully then boldly move in faith too.

There are two worlds good/bad and even if just a few the good will rescue/take you to success.

I'm the last to people-worship but I know this: in this system identity is trashed/we don't resist.

When strong she's the most dynamic of all but weak she's under his spell and is small/it's hell.

You let a guy take over your life when he didn't even deserve a conversation with you, aye.

SOUL MURDER

When I woke up I saw the rudiments: People in bad relationships and sick cyclic environments.

When I woke up I saw the rudiments: People in bad relationships and cyclic environments.

Germ phobia. Where you've been abused & traumatized you get real detailed on the other side.

Imagine yourself in a jet racing you away from the Philistines--the gross pigs of our day.

HE CALLS HIMSELF A "PLAYER"

You call yourself a "player" but buddy I see you as dirty. Contaminated, a haunted house and filthy.

So you do what any farm animal does and you feel special. It takes no strength to be a slut girl.

Why would any good woman wanna be with a man who brags about all the sex he had that cad.

I'm so sorry you had to go thru all that/endure that pig but it educates you so you'll be Mr. Big.

No matter how extreme those lessons you're tougher for them--the future is even brighter as elder.

He brags about all the sex he had with multitudes of women and you think anything of him?

Listen buddy what you're calling toxic femininity is just us protecting ourselves/being hep see.

Getting out of a soul tie relationship: Because it was fake to begin with you suddenly just hate it.

It's terrifying looking back at the close calls. Only God could have rescued you from a terrible fall.

SOUL MURDER

Show me my heart God and all my wicked thoughts then lead me in the everlasting path.

What are those ties driving you crazy? Sometimes it's deferred hope and it acts biochemically.

BREAK TIES TO TOXIC PEOPLE

You're tied to toxic people/narcissists thru deferred hope: he led you to believe fantasies of gold.

Even tho' they're now gone your soul is still tied because your hope is still planted: beseech God.

Hope deferred maketh the heart sick. He soul ties you by selling a dream then never fulfilling it.

I can sell you a dream but then withhold, then work thru a soul tie I've established in your soul.

It works the same as unforgiveness. As long as you can't forgive he's occupying soul space.

Forgive to free up space so that it instantly fills in with good things: grudges don't serve the ace.

Nothing takes up more space than a soul tie occupying all your thoughts until the demon dies.

That's why separation/recovery feels joyous: Finally free you feel you're riding happy waves.

These soul ties can go on for life unless we enlighten the deferred hope victim about this guy.

A life of deferred hope wrecks future relationships since you can't trust anyone now [brokenness].

Imagine: your fifteen years down the road but you're still tied to Harold thru broken hopes.

SOUL MURDER

Said in another way, the meanest people/things becoming strongholds blocking self-correction.

CARNIVORE EXPERIMENT: YUK!

To the clear chicken smells like fecal matter and is this cuz it now comes from China? I wonder.

No more carnivore diet cuz everyone's different. I got depressed/breathless and wanted out of it.

Fruit, leaves and a little cheese for protein. No more meat cuz of which I couldn't even breathe.

A scientist experiments on himself when it comes to food. I want my happy days back: fruit.

It works at first. Like any poison the first reactions are "higher" so you're hooked--the devil's device.

A sober alcoholic taking a drink again may feel 'higher" but then spirals down, sinking in the mire.

FIRST REACTION TO POISON IS GOOD

My first reaction to meat-eating resumption was I felt better than ever but soon went way under.

On my last day I slow-cooked chicken and the smells were so gross I was revolted/that ended it.

There were times I was so protein deficient all I thought of was chicken but cheese fixed this hon'.

Breathlessness brings the fear of suffocation and a panic. Right after beef, my self experiment.

Reaction to poisons: the body mind's reaction to trauma is to give you a little lift to deal with it:

SOUL MURDER

Johnny Depp is just an ordinary alcoholic: blackouts and the devil coming thru in absurd antics.

So much testimony/questioning about alcoholic bouts he can't recollect but are characteristic.

SUDDEN INTEREST IN NARCISSISM

Why so much on narcissism suddenly? It's about aging babies--an entire generation like you don't wanna be.

Man loves his sins and will do anything to maintain em until hitting bottom and it all turns around.

Until hitting bottom--on the way down--they act like aging babies and this includes most all of us, sad to say.

Not until you know how much you can lose, and how fast you can lose it, do you become an adult/mentally fit.

The kids of the nouveau riche are complacent and that leads to dissipation cuz they feel invincible.

I had to lose everything and live on a shoestring to learn the most important things, it's about priorities.

To learn simplicity and essentially I had to live in a tiny cabin then took only those few things to a mansion.

Then when I humbled myself [was humiliated] enough God gave me all and I moved on up--like a miracle.

BROUGHT UP IN A TINY CABIN

But the aging baby must learn a few things first. He has to undo every darn thing he's learned in this era.

Attraction, learn to take a step back. Attraction is just animal instinct but logic/reason is what we want.

SOUL MURDER

Not appreciating the value of home until they're in a situation where they see it shelters em from harm.

I split a 5" pizza with two dogs and we're all on high energy, buzzing around getting it all done.

Stop feeling remorse about when Satan had control. Anything can happen, everything did, so what.

A change of diet can change all hormones and psychology [personality] instantaneously and amazingly.

No matter what you did it's still just a demon, the NOT-YOU. I know it's hard to forget it though.

Forget Politix! My new life is music or movies as we spiral down or rise up and hopefully face our enemies.

You wouldn't talk that way to a child and a lady's no different. It was disgusting now that I think of it.

It's not that I'm choking by not acting, but because I have great patience I believe in going slow/waiting.

I'm not procrastinating or choking I'm simply and humbly waiting for God's direction honey.

Once the hero begins to spiral down in sin there comes a point where he can't stop--God hands him over son.

You deserve to have a life even though you screwed up. Thru' Jesus you get fresh start, clean slate, unstuck.

THRU JESUS A FRESH START

Before I knew Jesus I was so messed up. As they say I'd been around the block tho' just in my thoughts.

Church has slid so far away from sound doctrine that no one cares anymore, they make up their own religion.

SOUL MURDER

The churches keep moving into the beast of apostasy until it's overwhelming how far people are from God.

We have allowed children to be indoctrinated into witchcraft. How's that? Everything's about MAGIC.

TV AND THE OCCULT

TV IS OCCULT: Magic this, magic that--the toys are all about magic and I see signs of it even in the ads.

Freedom's why I'm here behind a wall and a gate and why I did everything to escape California a police state.

Soul sleep: Or do we go UP to heaven and come back down again into a grave so we can be raptured up?

Harry Potter isn't just a book, it's transformed the whole world cuz everything's about magic, a HOOK.

It isn't black vs. good magic--it's all bad: video games not knowing they're pulled into a Satanic world.

In the world of religion now everyone's an apostle. But we're reviled, persecuted, defamed, made filth.

TRUE APOSTLES WERE DESTITUTE

The true apostles were destitute but we follow and think the prosperity preachers are cute.

People send em money by the millions. They don't read the letters but people are hypnotized by them.

The new breed is saying "who needs stuffy doctrines/ bible preaching?" Cuz if not, you don't have anything.

When you admire Hollywood supermodels pretending to be religious you're giving into demons/feeling/emotion.

SOUL MURDER

Prosperity teachers are here to destroy souls leading money-hungry people to a devil's hell.

They teach getting rich is magic by giving them money to get the job done. But we go directly to the throne.

You don't need a prosperity preacher [PP] you need Jesus Christ. We are at the very last part of the church age.

Enemies of the cross of Christ who's god is their belly, glory is their shame and who mind earthly things.

ENEMIES OF THE CROSS

Rebellion against God's word is counted as witchcraft. They pierce themselves thru with many sorrows.

If you're not cold nor hot--lukewarm--God'll spew you outa His mouth. He doesn't want anything to do with ya.

All thru history when women felt called to preach they started new religions that weren't biblical, see?

Women are not to have spiritual authority over a man and when it's children they turn out even worse than.

"I fell out of love". No you didn't, you chose not to love your wife. It's a CHOICE or there's constant strife.

If they aren't diligent and creative themselves they'll blame you for neglecting them--they aren't busy elves.

I've had losers/couch potatoes get angry, even violent with me because I rejected/disinvited them supposedly.

They don't do anything with their time and sleep in. It's just disgustin' so don't have anything to do with em.

I didn't put em up there to sell em--that's not how I make a livin'. They're my only legacy to those left standin'.

SOUL MURDER

After a certain age one fears engulfment or loss of identity. It's happened, so put things back on simmer, see?

Fearing engulfment by a bottomless pit or a deep cavern: that's the feeling in an experienced older person.

It takes you down a rabbit hole and you don't know what they're gonna do-- hurt again by a jerk/a shrew.

FEELING IMPOSED ON

Feeling imposed on: like they wanted a piece of me--that's how I instantly felt, please let me be!

The minute I was around em they eyed me like a hungry tiger, searching me out, what can I get from her?

The women were equally bad--all wanting something or borrowing. I just hate that, I want solitude honey.

In any room space I feel encroached upon by rapacious amoral youth but you were in your fifties, dude.

They don't know a thing but they want what you have. It's a sucking spirit, whether they need it or not.

They come into your house and outright ask: can I have this, can I have that? These are children, brats.

And it's all due to the communist spirit taught in the schools: they deserve it cuz you got more, fools.

Like a very young child, they come into your house and want everything. They want your life/fantasy.

They come into your home and bring their friends without asking. You don't get a chance to vet--that's hating.

The Social comes first so if you don't accept ruffians you're a hater and being asocial is an "anxiety disorder".

SOUL MURDER

So the communist spirit allows them to take your things and bring their friends--we're all one, earthlings.

If you don't like "his friends" you're a hater and this could be a violence-inciter. Watch, beware!

Since they're all cut from the same cloth they go along with those things which you despise and are abhorrent.

Porn addiction is all about withdrawn attention. Life is a pie and you just became a much smaller piece.

NEED A LOCKED GATE

It took a lifetime to realize I even needed a wall and a locked gate. I was naive and loving: bad fate.

There is similitude to each generation. That's the bell-shaped curve, the herd, social acculturation.

It may spread to homosexuality from porn. It makes sense that it would generalize--no lines about a thing.

A continual dropping on a rainy day and a contentious woman are alike. Prov 27: 15. Drip, drip, drip.

Women shouldn't talk to other women's husbands because this is the setup for affairs, you've seen em.

Woman should stay in the home to prevent this or stay with women--except then the divorcees influence em.

A woman should obey her husband not take instructions from another man cuz that triggers her emotions.

Don't remorse over wasted years. Life is short, suddenly it's over so with all your heart love the Lord.

One little word, one raised eyebrow, looking at a woman a little too long--its all it takes/she's back in his face.

SOUL MURDER

I was banned by the feminist moderator for the most obtuse, obscure, far-fetched, ridiculous reason.

Investigative behaviors triggered by betrayal trauma ARE our mal-adaptive illness but so what, we gotta do it.

Not a wizard I've just done my homework.

They were crazy and their demons got on you then you became even worse until it ran it's course.

How could Paris Syndrome be a mental illness when Paris really IS filled with violence, trash and rudeness?

Betrayed wives are always so happy when things are stable and predictable. But then, outa the blue....

Paul was so shocked how they were using a corrupt gospel of adding WORKS to grace and works to faith.

When Paul saw the churches adding WORKS to faith and grace he called them "bewitched"--enslavement.

A big change is coming--remember whether good or bad change causes stress: mind your diet/sleeping.

WORKS DOCTRINES FAIL

Start adding WORKS to faith/grace and it's never enough. Drip drip drip, your church becomes rot/all fluff.

Works are never enough, don't you see? You slide into boredom/lethargy, you've lost the fire though its free.

Paul got real nervous seeing the new churches adding WORKS to the gospel when the CROSS settles it all.

WORKERS ARE BEWITCHED

True believers, bewitched? How could this happen Paul chagrined. It's very simple: adding WORKS to them.

24

SOUL MURDER

It was always the same: I'd have a spiritual awakening and join a church who'd load me up with stuff inane.

And if I didn't want their boring socials they'd accuse me of rejecting God--imagine the arrogance that entailed.

The works church is also part of the world. Abortion and homosexuality is slowly becoming their new order.

After being saved by grace--for free, so cool--why go back into church enslavement and a system of rules?

Rules, ceremonies, rituals, socials--I got so sick of it all! Inside I knew this wasn't God, it was worldly HELL.

Salvation by bewitchers is ALWAYS works. Works is the bewitching lie that kills the good people in church.

Satan counterfeits the true gospel so there's just enough truth to ensnare the naive and keep em in the pews.

STOP DICTATING

Stop telling me I gotta do this/gotta do that, I gotta go here/gotta go there. Leave me be--God is my Father.

How humans pervert things--and the gospel is the best example. We need true gospel sheepherders too.

The GOOD NEWS is your new life/fresh start is FREE and you don't do a thing but love Jesus and believe.

It's a PERSON not a set of rules. It's a lamp to guide not a brick to carry--that's Satan not your heavenly daddy.

In the false church Ms. Social Charm becomes a respected elder, not for loving the gospel but for being popular.

I believe in terseness and laconic alacrity so don't write long letters and don't over-explain--spit it out, ok?

SOUL MURDER

So boring/senseless--no wonder the churches fell. Paul's greatest concern was them becoming an empty shell.

HOMILECTICS: ART OF PREACHING

I can't preach but I do teach preachers [HOMILETICS]. I tell them: hold to the line/don't deviate one bit.

When women rule the church it's all about false issues, emotions and signaling but men maintain reality.

I couldn't believe it when the rulish snobs ok-ed abortion and homos. These were the elders too ya know.

No wonder dad didn't like going to church anymore, no wonder he popped a beer coming thru the door.

Even the worst sinner would be fascinated if the TRUE gospel was preached cuz with new eyes, he'd see.

When a church becomes so lukewarm and compromised like that it becomes fascistic with Jezebel splits.

Every single new testament warning about false doctrine is the assumption true believers can be bewitched!

FAKES ARE ARROGANT AND MEAN

They're arrogant and mean in their falseness which is always compensatory causing anger and rudeness.

Every command to hold on to Truth was based on the saints' susceptibility to being bewitched, get it?

I wasn't bewitched I was just bored. If the true gospel is preached it's so exciting and enlivening I soar.

When they say "I don't believe the gospel" that's obvious. The bewitching part is: "need works to be saved".

SOUL MURDER

Paul was saying "when I'm gone you'll be hit inside and out, to change the gospel to WORKS, that's all".

She took me to her boring church and they had hands in the air spouting pagan songs and slogans, I declare.

CHURCHES AND LEADERS BEWITCHED

Most churches and leaders are bewitched. They believe the core gospel but have allowed adulterants.

The bewitching goes to high levels. Go to a Christian book store--you can't trust all those popular titles.

The true gospel is simple enough for a child to understand but they make it complex filled with works adulterants.

John said all that matters is his children walking in truth--so with all those false teachers have nothing to do.

People at high levels and preachers you hear don't know the minimum requirements to be saved--weird.

To "bewitch" is to fascinate and charm in a misleading way. That's your guy, a new trinket or the church today.

Social engines just turn off your counter so you don't know who's looking and they aren't getting em either.

QUESTION INTENSE ATTRACTIONS

Intense attractions and feelings: watch these! Take control, don't be the victim of alluring sirens.

For that alluring siren that's exploding in your attractions may turn out to be an illusion for your destruction.

The bewitcher seeks to do harm to one by his lies, deception and false promises: HARM, distress.

SOUL MURDER

It's not so much what's happened to nonbelievers, but to believers--not by sorcery/spells but false doctrine.

Never interrupt your enemy when they're destroying themselves. Napoleon Bonaparte

BE SWEPT UP BY GOD NOT MAN

I don't like things that are bigger than I am--like I'm swooped up. I'm pulled by God, He fills my cup.

I can't allow myself to be swept off my feet by you. I will fight this thing because self-control is a fruit.

I will fight these feelings and emotions to the end because I've learned they're not my friend/I'll ignore em.

We wanna be PULLED by God not SWEPT UP--off our feet, down another street, the self depleted, effete.

The younger women activated his traumatic memories and used his own insecurities against him.

I can hear someone yelling/screaming at me inside. That's an introject--swallowed whole tho' they died.

I can't go all fruit cuz I"m always hungry/low energy. I was brought up on dairy but just one meal, amazing.

Pizza gets the job done, that's all. It's for us workers and that means energy, creativity--make it habitual.

We have to eat right? So it's good to settle on something, get the elements in and agree to a good routine.

SOUL MURDER

Attachment Traumas and Social Hypnotism

Declare this to the whole world: You WILL not do this to me, I will take control because now I am whole.

WICKED MEN WORMING THEIR WAY IN

Wicked men worming their way into your house and you feel joyous cuz you're so needy boss?

Sometimes one is tied thru perversion. Pushing beyond her comfort zone now becomes a bond.

He pushes, she settles for that. He pushes more and each time he's more entrenched in her soul.

Lust plays itself off as love but love is fulfilled and lust is never is. Love has limits, lust never sis.

As he pushes further and you accept, your values degenerate and you're cheap/far from perfect.

A stronghold has developed around sex. A powerful seducer and all she thinks about, a hex.

SEEING YOURSELF AS WORTHELSS

She begins to see herself as worth less then worthless: used goods undeserving of decentness.

SOUL MURDER

The way she perceives herself as a result of imposed perversion makes it impossible to move on.

Sometimes she's tied thru insecurities. Her identity and values are purely in her relationship see.

You found your social circle with him & your identity's all in so when he's gone you're mentally ill.

Her whole identity was her connection to that person, never thinking to plan for when he's gone.

TRAUMA THE SOUL BINDER

The big soul binder is trauma. He's hurt you so much he's locked in your soul replacing mama.

Ask God to reveal where the tie is: hope deferred, insecurities, perverse, traumatic: what is it.

Once finding what level the tie is on, ask the holy spirit to remove in you what's not right with God.

Ask God to uproot everything that is not righteous--repenting for your part [sin] in the process.

Yes you had your early trauma reasons but you must repent for making a god out of a person.

Some traumatized women move right into whore status to survive, it's like a last ditch effort, aye.

You must repent for your role in the folie a deux so the saving grace/holy spirit can finally move.

Fully repented the holy spirit washes everything out that God did not put there, from a cultural war.

FIND AREA, ASK GOD TO CLEAN IT OUT

SOUL MURDER

Seeing the areas a soul tie compromised you turn to the mighty power of God to break the bondage.

Was it a weird sex attraction gluing you to a guy on youtube? Find the area for God to pursue.

Don't complicate the process with religious rites or hollering chants, just ask God to commence.

Keep focus on yourself: cutting this dirty thing out of you so easily taken in by predator stealth.

AVOID ALLEY CATS

Why would you be with an alley cat who'd been with so many women, are you nuts or a masochist?

Was it insecurity making you lay down so easily? The psychopath would make you homeless see.

Was it deferred hope? Give up fantasy dope cuz it's never gonna happen it's just his way ya' know.

Did he bring so much crap into your psychic map his strangling hex has brought on a collapse?

Has he brought on moral collapse due to perversion push? Have you accepted it/values bashed?

These are the four areas enabling soul ties. If you investigate thoroughly on God you can rely.

Are you traumatized and that's why you stay? It'll only get worse as sadism always increases ok.

This was my prayer down in the mire: God I need you, this is beyond me, rescue me from a liar!

MR. BIG IS A PUNY LITTLE MAN

SOUL MURDER

When finally released from this creep you will see that Mr. Big was such a little man/evil stink.

Making a god out of someone is the outcome of an evil stronghold invading and making you dumb.

For the sinner worships man not God: the creature not the Creator of it all, and thus his fall.

Man-worship is a sorry punishment for laying down in weakness, a life of missed opportunities.

The culture has replace people-worship for God, see our adoration of pop culture and Hollywood.

In a social generation being social is seen as a requirement for salvation--what an evil notion.

ASK GOD TO REMOVE IT ALL, EVEN SOCIAL

Asking God to remove all that was not Him I felt no more social obligation to such boredom.

I've been soul tied and know the feeling: being in a prison of confusion and pain with the unloving.

Jumping into a new relationship to escape then having the same process happen again, ole.

If you must transfer to someone new at least find a nice man you can really trust and rely on too.

God forgive us for things we allowed & those we created on our own. It's embarrassing. I know.

Once entrenched in your soul the lecherous man can literally drag you thru the mud like a slut.

It's a lot to come to terms with, memories of how you were used by that snake so venomous.

SOUL MURDER

As this point it helps to relate to all women, a sisterhood completely aware of this sexual hypnotism.

And here's the stronghold: I'm just a worthless slut and don't deserve a nice man so here I sit/yuk!

From discussion above the value of chastity reveals itself–keeping daughters safe from stealth.

Sex is the biggest binder, that's how couples stay together, but perversion takes us under.

HE BROUGHT YOU UNDER

Your situation would stay virtuous had it not been for his stealth obnoxious so go easy on yourself sis.

God made me so tough I won't let a man in my house without chaperoned, that's the result.

God, he's created a bondage in my soul and Father I need you now, save me from his undertow.

For YOU are my Father and Creator, not this lecherous faker who's just on the take/a manipulator.

When finally free of his evil control you must forgive it all SO THAT he no longer occupies your soul.

Ask God to remove the self-destructive bent that [like a magnet] goes for whoremongers & maggots.

A dam narcissist who puts himself out as the mostess but is just an old alley cat chasing skirts sis.

Repent, ask God to return factory settings then marry a nice man and be good to him miss.

MARRYING EX-ALLEY CATS

SOUL MURDER

If you want to marry an ex-alley cat be extra sure of him or he'll revert to crap and sink in his swill.

Take my word for it, don't go on wasting one more minute. Write it off for the lesson is infinite.

He's so proud of his sexual prowess, acting like any goat, cat, dog, cow or any animal of course.

Little Man is so puny in character he's got to control you to feel any power but it never stops there.

He's a disgusting little jerk putting himself first [you could never be a husband or daddy sir].

Just knowing the unforgiven take up too much space in your noggin allows you to forgive them.

DEFINE YOURSELF OR SOMEONE WILL

Poor kid her mom's a malignant narcissist and like all liberals accuses her of what she does.

If a woman does not define herself she will be defined by someone else and that will be rough.

You cannot be defined by someone else and by the same token you should not obsess.

If incapable of finding definition/peace within yourself you'll never find it with someone else.

If you obsess--your center of gravity way over on another person--you can say "I'm not healthy".

If you ascribe value to yourself due to connection to another you know you have work to do sir.

Your children/spouse/job could be gone. There are two giving you identity inside: you and God.

SOUL MURDER

"Silly women" allow the world to conform them to a miniature version of who they are: below par.

A QUEEN FUNCTIONING AS A SLAVE

Tho' they are queens they function like slaves and it's such a shame watching all of em degrade.

And the perverted male society sniffs them out and takes advantage of them every time.

If you "can't make it without a man" you have serious work to do: find your SELF and repent.

The demonic force plants the lie that you'll never survive without a certain guy--that's a wish to die.

With weakness a spirit of codependency desires to shift the focus from God to man: damned.

This is why it is so important to get an identity before relationship. Don't trigger that sick spirit.

If you're "dying" to be with or think only of him rather than your own thing that's a soul tie man.

Part of the dying part is he's not interested, triggering the early attachment trauma with momma.

OBSESSIVE UNREQUITED LOVE

Obsessive unrequited love relationships are hell and reduplicate the early trauma [rings a bell].

This demonic spirit causes one to make a god of another but when he falls watch out brother.

Many biblical characters symbolize the mentality of one oppressed by a spirit of codependency.

SOUL MURDER

This same spirit goads us to "wait" on other people to deliver us when it's God inside every one of us.

You can't control if one enters or stays in your life. That's the thing, codependency's not right.

Obsessive fascination with a man is people-worship, putting man above God and its demonic.

SHIFT focus to Self. Get into your divine talents unique to you and tell that "love" spirit to go to hell.

For you don't "love" him you're libidinally attracted by a demonic soul tie which is always sexual doll.

A soul tie is always sexual and an obsessive gruesome twosome is too: a trauma bond of coo coo.

LOVE CRUTCHES AND ADDICTIONS

You must avoid this and question all attractions. Then take things slow to avoid predispositions.

For narcissism is the personality of today. They love bomb then discard--throw you all away.

That feeling in the gut--of nausea, pain, shame, panic--is from upset in your emotional environment.

He triggered early trauma with momma or poppa and now you're in a panic looking for mana.

Food, booze, sex--mana from heaven--is only temporary and hell-bound but curable with wisdom.

We adapt to our environment which now has a flood of unwanted emotions in it: seek God quick.

Crutches are ameliorative without being panaceac--temporal--but eternal comes from the moral.

SOUL MURDER

Worship God your father and allow bad men to FADE and to fade quickly as a mirage of leaven.

DO YOUR WORK NOW ATTRACT THE ONE

Dream of someone who loves your work and is decent. Do your work, get perfect, now he's sent.

You can have him. He's not interested in a thing you have to say but acts like he is: no fun.

Never sweat someone who was a mirage to begin with: A soul tie from early trauma & wish to die.

He could fit into a keyhole if he wanted to--that's an actor but also the narcissist, 1000 selves.

And don't trust his recent upgrades cuz he's likely to reverse from that or go on some tangent.

BE IN CONTROL OF YOUR SOUL

All you control is your own soul, defined within yourself or be forever pegged by someone else.

So he hoovers back after discard--so what? Don't forget that, the hurt and pain from that rat.

Happiness attained at the expense of virtue is shortlived and shallow. It means your excellence is low.

Thru media she thinks she must be a certain way to be acceptable to people who don't matter.

A queen performing for congregation of clowns. When champagne fun night's over she's down.

Now you see what you've given up--virtue, excellence--for nothing, a roll in the hay with scum.

Happiness attained at expense of virtue is short lived & painful too as self-disgust makes one blue.

SOUL MURDER

Dollars are gone but when virtue is shattered you have to live with that including nightmares.

There are ways that seemeth right to a queen but the end are ways of death [guilt and shame].

MIRTH/PARTYING FOLLOWED BY SORROW

Even in laughter the heart is sorrowful and the end of that mirth is heaviness: you feel it miss.

After taking selfies for instagram your heart is heavy and sorrowful: that's modern life in a bowl.

Heaviness, depression: that's how it always ends and who needs that—a predictable situation.

How many times did you compromise your virtue and it always ended in that PIT of depression?

How many times did you compromise your virtue then it ended in that PIT of depression too?

Self-awareness is surely the biggest determinant of living a consistent, stable, successful life.

If you KNOW your standards, boundaries and limitations you don't get close to that fire again man.

You don't get close to the fire cuz you know the aftermath: the horrible guilt, the hangover.

You will disappoint others but shake your head if you disappoint yourself and God/all that matters.

MATURITY IS SELF-AWARENESS

Maturity is understanding there are certain things you cannot get away with or you speed dying.

There is no good coming from it whatsoever and any thrills from it are not gonna last mister.

SOUL MURDER

When you compromise and accept less than you know you deserve you fall into self abuse.

The inability to reject less than I deserve is an invitation to self-abuse. Need assertion training too.

ONCE YOU accept less, the price keeps dropping. It's incremental falling into low self-esteem.

Once you start to put up with stuff, where's the nonnegotiable now? Energy drops low.

LIKE MOM SAID LIFE'S A BITCH

As mom said, life's a bitch. But thru knowledge of social psych you overcome it/make it rich.

Greek tragedies are all about families. People are the problem and they're the closest see.

Families are great and I truly believe in them but they're also the cause of mental illness son.

Ok you've been through all this. Now enjoy life by not continuously and agonizingly reliving it.

To be extraordinary makes them hate you. You gotta be a blob or something they're used to.

Key to success is not-acting. Let it well up in you until God puts you in the light/endless spring.

When you get close to leaving the earth sooner than later you see things differently altogether.

IF YOU'RE SMART THEY HATE YOU

With illiteracy increasing if you're smart they hate your guts. It's the Dunning-Kruger Effect folks.

SOUL MURDER

There's no more respect, no more civility and with this manufactured depression they're angry.

You are beyond hope/therapy, there is no other answer but to separate from thee.

She gave up her Christian heritage then married and became a Hindu and then a commie too.

To be great is pure. Passion, energy, enthusiasm to create, anticipate: living for the arts sir.

Of course I shudder looking back but I also know life is a ladder with some painful lessons in fact.

I have wisdom cuz I've been hurt. It pierced the mystic center as I entered an entirely new world.

REPENT then prepare for mass attractions to the true self, the Philosopher's Stone, the elf.

Not getting his way he pulled the nuclear option and an immature man had an embarrassing tantrum.

The word "nice" in Latin means "ignorant" and "naive". That's exactly what it means down deep.

THE PROBLEM IS ALWAYS PEOPLE

The problem is always people. Think about it: you're happy then they start up and are critical.

They didn't know you had a mental illness they just saw you as a jackass cuz it looks the same as.

Narcissists are kings of imperative thinking: you've got to, you must, can't, should, supposed to.

He can't change--he's paralyzed with input--so pushes his dysfunction around making us all nuts.

SOUL MURDER

I'm Scotch, I love privacy. If I could I'd have a locked gate, fighting dogs and a moit around me.

Trauma brings collapsed morals & boundaries then she started drinking to self-medicate see.

When they saw I wanted it they wanted it too & even pooled their resources to push it through.

With any business deal, talk to no one. No bar room bragging or someone brings obstruction.

For your victory: trust no one, move point by point, do everything perfectly, pray constantly.

Once you wake up its easy to become a misogynist but then comes the hardest part: forgiveness.

If you don't have FIRM boundaries the evil world comes in like a tidal wave whether girl or old lady.

They are familial and family creates mental illness & meanness when the situation calls for it.

If members are mentally ill it's "folie a famille" which is sicker than folie a deux: gruesome twosome.

SYSTEMS OF DYSFUNCTION LAST

After leaving she had to play out mental illness for two decades until the readaptation took place.

You can't have the kind of success I'm talking about without a Waterloo too: see it like that.

Instead of remorsing over the past thank God you had the constant mess make you the best.

I want solitude/privacy and you've been busting my boundaries honey so this is it: caio, bye.

SOUL MURDER

Escaping Borrego: Making it Outa Small Town Hell. That was the key to my success after all.

The narcissist is marked by his imperatives: you've got to, you must, you're supposed to you nut.

The desert was so wonderful but the small town neurosis was stressful, close, unescapable.

You saw your friggin' foes at the post office where we got our mail. That kinds friggin' thing ok.

It was like a black cloud following me around. Just when I was healed they'd open another wound.

I guess being hot makes you mean. It was 125 degrees at times but I never saw anything like it see.

They were so mean and the women were the worst. They sized up the new girl in town, cursed.

I tried to escape into churches but then the church ladies would come by to criticize, oh my.

But I wrote about the Small Town Neuroses in 130 books so you see I turned it into good.

It was like a prison that way. These weren't a buncha rentals it was an inescapable mazeway.

THEY SIZE YOU UP & GOSSIP

They size you up then you divide into groups for protection but then that's more deception.

He doesn't know what he's talking about but still everything is "must", "got to", "supposed to/should".

Many men offer the woman escape in this predicament but careful, it's just another encumbrance.

SOUL MURDER

I got so prickly sensitive even a mean look would send me into terror, the total load was way over.

A small town surrounded by mountains: all we had was each other and it was sickening brother.

Gossip rules in a small town. Often pure fabrication ruins your rep as it makes the rounds.

So she escaped into the arms of the fat hardware store owner then a horse rancher, both abusers.

As even her lower companions left her she even hoped a gang of juvenile boys would save her.

This was the story of humiliation: extreme humbling in public as they all join in the killing.

They get so bored & restless in the hot desert they can't wait to chime in with unpleasantness.

As even her lower companions left her she yet hoped a gang of juvenile boys would protect her.

When a gang of boys are your only "friends" the catty women in town go wild with that one.

These lower companions/bad associations wanted everything I had. Borrowers, users, cads.

SPIRALING DOWN PROCESS

This is the spiraling down process of sinners: a downward pull made far worse by the others.

People live in an alternative universe and they're at the center. When they lack empathy, it's over.

It's almost hard to imagine how dense they are in their thinking especially when adding narcissism.

SOUL MURDER

To avoid this severe undertow your new slogan must be Hold Your Head Up High or it's baby byebye.

It's hardly uplifting to be around someone who is highly controlling. Women, men, kids are guilty.

Or they're so self-impressed they step over you to elevate themselves, that's the narcissist.

ENDGAME THOUGHTS

My goal is to be the most famous writer of this century said the desert rat in a shack with nothing.

I just wanna write and talk--that's all--until i've passed on to eternity talking only to my God.

I don't do anything for money but a tenfold increase comes mysteriously back to me: godly.

Slow, stable and steady the turtle wins the race. That's daily work tho' tedious til you've aced.

I guess i'm a writer cuz that's all I do day and night sir. It's the songs of a singer/works of a painter.

PROSPERITY AND RESTORED YOUTH

Evil falls but the righteous will prosper in everything they do as their youth is restored like the eagle.

Depedestalization is sad cuz it means all doors closed to further opportunity-- over the hill they say.

You can't stop their fall. Things are determined by God and they did it--they refused to repent/hear His call.

You turned a beautiful opportunity into something dirty and that's the end for you man/pray for mercy.

SOUL MURDER

It makes no difference how much money someone has sin will pull them down and they'll be blocked, yah.

It doesn't matter who you know, sin will pull you down. There's no strength in numbers, it's God.

Your mutual admiration society is pathetic. All for the fans but what would happen if she was a lunatic?

I don't know if I can go on your show. Are you the LINK? I have to be led by God, I'm waiting to know.

When getting clear you can reach back and change the past. Einstein said it's all a dimension/gas.

He/she didn't ruin your life, your decision to have sex outa marriage ruined your life by created strife.

MIXED SIGNALS FROM FRENEMIES

It's the mixed signals from frenemies that causes us to detach from our truth and our very destiny.

I cut off everyone but my husband and I felt so much better. People really are a hindrance sister.

For success be more discerning about people. They hold you back, they question your philosophy/morals.

Toxic people have two faces and that's how they get into your good graces especially if rich/famous.

They're gonna change, know that. It's like taking a drink if you're an alcoholic, you can't EVER predict it.

I see him puffing himself up but without true substance. No foundation just common herd sense.

NO EMPATHY/PATHOLOGICAL ENVY

SOUL MURDER

You found out the hard way when learning there are people with no empathy PLUS pathological envy.

It's our sins vs. purity that determines how we age. Everyone's cute at first, it's in stages.

He'd been handsome but then aged in a really weird way reflecting his sins/appetites of his latter days.

Like the devil this narcissist has a thousand faces and can be whatever he wants to fit different cases.

One day God pulled the plug on his beauty and oh my, what a drastic change-- it was really ugly.

So to compensate [save himself] he talked about sex since sex sells but the backlash kicked him into hell.

First she played victim then became a bully, the nastiest. Female narcissists are malignant and dangerous.

The more public her smear campaign the happier she is. The more humiliating, the better her image.

Narcissists will do anything to win--any sabotaging, any cruel thing. That is why you must cut the chain.

It's quite a revelation to see how MANY are narcissists and this is why we learn about em: it protects.

Narcissism exploded in the sixties when everything was now "me, me, me" in hedonistic sensuality.

I became terrified of her flying monkeys. She was so damaged she was compelled to get em after me.

She's a malignant narcissist because she'd been hurt but that revelation doesn't remove the curse.

Malignant female narcissists use sex to increase control for longer periods-- her men are her military.

SOUL MURDER

NARC FEMALES ALWAYS ENVY, *ALWAYS*

Malignant narcissists always envy--get that--and they always take revenge thru flying monkeys.

She uses sex to control men and will withdraw it if need be. She'll sleep with your husband, she has no loyalty.

Her one desire is to WIN and that means your destruction. She is so dam dangerous, cut her loose man.

If you love your dog she'll kill your dog. These things happen but you never connect the dots.

Men were dangerous to me but women were shrewdly underhanded with [hitmen] flying monkeys.

If rich they'll use lawyers to do their dirty work or they'll call your relatives to cause you more hurt.

IF YOU KNOW A WOMAN LIKE THIS

If you know a woman like this you must disengage because she has no conscience and will do the worst.

I'd never do that--I'm no match for the malignant narcissist. If tangled up, get out fast cuz she's dangerous.

You would never, ever do the things she does to people. You're no match--must separate from evil.

Since it's her flying monkeys doing the dastardly deeds you must quickly do everything you can to secede.

What makes women so dangerous is they collude together for advice and it's always anti-common sense.

Especially if a target is good looking they ALL wanna do her in for adulterous generations are filled with envy.

SOUL MURDER

There are movies made on this and they're frightening as hell--like when a whole school hates one girl.

A mother is so jealous of her daughter she talks her down in total humiliation to anyone who will listen.

I just wanted to be alone and this they took as rejection and became really mean even in my home.

THEY HATE YOU SUDDENLY

Overnight, the Jews were hated. A social matrix can turn on a dime: it's study is called Social Psychology.

Suddenly, they all hated me. I had said/done something that changed the matrix making me the enemy.

No matter what she does it's "I've done nothing wrong". Her versions of this are limitless/shameless.

Malignant narcissists don't feel guilt nor shame, just pathological ENVY of other people.

The Female Malignant Narcissist is Pathologically Envious of Other People: that's all you gotta know.

They don't have feelings of empathy but ELECTRIC levels of envy, the most dangerous of all frenemies.

The covert narcissist's behavior is far more timid and concealed but he's just as much a heel.

The covert lacks the big, aggressive, bold behaviors of the overt narcissist-- coming off as gentle/honest.

The overt may offend without guilt/never apologize but the covert wants approval/will cover everything up.

Don't search for past actors they're just archetypes being played out, the players themselves irrelevant.

SOUL MURDER

LIBERALISM AND NARCISSISM

Liberalism has encouraged and taught narcissism. It's the default setting and it's opposite to humility.

Narcissistic malignant females get with lawyers in the divorce business to destroy men's lives.

They take them to the cleaners, they put them thru a ringer. It is hell on earth to divorce, a killer.

As divorce starts the sea parts and the whole world takes her side--that's historically where we are.

The covert's always offering help in times of need but is never around when you need them, see?

Covert narcs will pit people against each other, always in underhanded ways like gossip-called-concern.

They act concerned but it's just a way to get information. They ask pointed questions and note it son.

Your own sister will drop bad seeds of information about you knowing it'll cause problems too.

All narcissists bore very easily so love to incite chaos and drama. Gossip is their tool and it can kill ya.

I got rid of one Jezebel only to get another in a housekeeper who was equally a homewrecker.

I feel so much happier not thinking of you all the time. Whew--what an obsession was mine.

Hidden narcissism: passive-aggression, sneakiness with abuse tactics but not impossible to detect.

VIRTUE SIGNALING IS NOT MORALITY

SOUL MURDER

They conflate virtue signaling with morality. They feel superior, I can tell by their approach to me.

They get a little restless and start to create trouble. It's the image of the Hippopotamus in a female.

Having adapted to a bad dad, when things get too tranquil they gotta create trouble to feel at home.

Not thinking of you all the time--and suffering--I have all that mental space back and Mr. it is so fine.

Dad always told me to not let people take up too much space in the mind of an intellect, it's a fact.

An unhappy or sick relationship will destroy your talents and fine mind. It did mine when I was blind.

The first half of life was getting educated and overcoming the female relationships I was born into.

It's these people--the ones closest--that are eclipsing the true self in most cases. It takes years to resist.

In some cases they literally have to die to allow upstarts to finally find personal success: what a mess.

Especially with older [jealous] females who will not relent in targeting those for destruction, like Trump.

When it comes to enemies she's relentless, tenacious, focused, electrified: don't fight, just escape.

Narcissist mothers, for example, lack boundaries completely. She reveals secrets/reads diaries.

SHE GOSSIPS FOR CONTROL

I feel the joy of someone who's excruciating pain has suddenly stopped. All about you, a nut.

SOUL MURDER

To stop her ruthless gossiping I'd cower before her, for to displease her meant she'd ruin me forever.

God knew I was writing out a new social psychology so He put me thru events regarding human treachery.

You are discarded for three reasons: he's bored, he's got better supply elsewhere or you're onto him.

When in the desert I felt imposed on anytime I met anyone and couldn't wait to get back to the cabin.

It wasn't that the mother misled her but the schools misled her and mom was too weak to curb her.

With trauma I developed PTSD and lost all meaning but then I found it in Jesus, nature, privacy.

I found meaning in the sound of rain on a tin roof or the sense of vastness in the desert: eternal lift.

Sorry you tried for meaning thru society--you really lost it buddy, reflected in your looks unfortunately.

BECAUSE YOU GET NO MEANING

Because you get no meaning from your fancied association with her or him. It's an inner journey and trip.

The perpetrator of complex PTSD is one closest. Imagine that, like being tortured while tied to a post.

What is the biggest result on the personality from trauma? TOXIC SHAME: ashamed of who I am/damned.

I lost all sense of protection and comfort. Love associated with abuse and the mind's on cruise.

PTSD blocks normal development even neurologically. Trauma: there are missing parts to his personality.

SOUL MURDER

Sometimes the mind on cruise means a huge blackout about what they are doing while addicting.

This personality blackout is called anosognosia, the loss of pattern recognition or ability for correction.

Complex PTSD blocks success in interpersonal relationships: after trauma they can't bond/trust.

INCONSISTENT REINFORCEMENT

Kind and nice at times, cruel and mean at times. This inconsistent reinforcement is the crime.

Emotional flashbacks: Experiencing the same emotion as during the trauma, overwhelming mental attacks.

I heard how he talked to another man when he didn't know I was listening and it turned my stomach.

She let loose on me so bad it didn't matter her apology later, I saw the devil and will never forget her.

When you say "NO" it causes narcissistic injury since he sees you as an extension of himself honey.

To Sir: I'm so glad to be over you and that this situation has passed, my perception is now so VAST!

I see you for what you are and it only took me forty years but I'm so much wiser after all those tears.

NO = narc injury since he's incapable of seeing you as a separate person with your own needs sweetie.

You need to TEST. Can this new guy meet your needs, respect your boundaries–does he raise his voice?

My boundaries were constantly pushed/tested but keeping distance brought anger from the herd of stupids.

SOUL MURDER

THEY HATE YOUR BOUNDARIES

I was constantly saying NO, NO, NO. That reminded them of their mother and violence easily took over.

I shoulda just shut the door rather than stand there arguing with him about why I didn't wanna let him in.

It scared me being "owned" by them--they were aghast I had my own boundaries and other plans.

The Mormons felt they owned me--I was to go to their boring socials not pursue my destiny at home.

When people think they own you they'll get violent often indirectly thru vicious, dangerous gossip.

People are like sticky quicksand to me. I stay clear but God said we'd have ONE friend/home with hubby.

I had two feminist sisters who sought to banish me from the earth so I've walked in your shoes Mister.

Young boys were enraged when I said NO and I thought they were gonna kill me--come Lord!

MAKING FUN OF YOUR NEEDS

The narcissist will hate your boundaries and make fun of your needs, especially to their flying monkeys.

I grew afraid to state my needs--like never come without calling first--to prevent troubles without cease.

I lived in this low class social matrix to write these books about how we're held down by narcissists.

These boundaries would fit a hardy frontier matrix but not the social generation after WWII/conformist.

SOUL MURDER

Boundaries, boundaries, boundaries--she's crazy! But soon after you'll see the results are amazing.

I live in a beautiful loving world of cats and dogs and NO human act can follow that--that's where I'm at.

NARCISSISTIC INJURY/PUSHBACKS

If you say to the narc "don't bring your friend" he'll do it again cuz he hates your boundaries man.

Narcs have agendas and if you NO it he'll treat you poorly/go silent--how dare you be independent.

Always stay in tune with your own thoughts/feelings and stand up for them-- with narcs it's prohibited.

If it's a good person he'll make adjustments, talk it out, take responsibility but narcs will gaslight, blame, escape.

Only now as I enter the final stage do I have perfect privacy to voice rage without imposers on the sage.

ONLY AFTER marriage and loving protection from a husband could my life's work blossom.

Always escaping people, fighting their resistances and nursing my wounds: finally, it's over/I'm alone.

IT TAKES A LIFE TO REALIZE

It took a life to realize I had to relocate and get a home with land and a locked gate to change my fate.

Home on land with locked gate is the greatest luxury cuz every moment's divinely mine--I create it honey.

I never answer phones as a terrible interruption but people seem to hate that- -they wanna talk a ton.

SOUL MURDER

My reality was no more rooted in dysfunctional relating, attachment trauma or disappointment.

You get used to grief and it's all you know so assume the past is what the future holds.

I finally realized: I don't have to grieve all the time or orient to intense loss, I can be boss.

The ChiComs are the cutout for globalist plans for us. Cruel, austere evil in total social conformity, yuk.

FROM ABUSE TO BEAUTIFUL VIEWS

I endured a life of relational abuse but now I'm behind a wall in exquisite beauty with gorgeous views.

Instead of being committed to solving the problem, commit instead to separating from it fast hon'.

NO ONE seems to understand the abuse you went thru. Pastors, counselors just don't get it, pooh!

I'd rather be beaten up with bruises than this slow-burn through the years of shit-shots and ridicule.

It's the little remarks that accumulate and drive you crazy as NO ONE SEES what's going on, not really.

DRIP DRIP DRIP DEVALUATION

Weeks, months, YEARS being devalued through the drip treatment. Drip, drip, drip combined with neutral.

It's so subtle and hidden NO one sees it except you. You start to talk about him for true reality held onto.

Well you endured so much it deteriorated you. It slowly changed your personality/you're always blue.

SOUL MURDER

Your soul is broken from constant never-ending drips of this stuff. Like the wife of the alcoholic, enough!

The wolf tricked you into his den where he pulled you apart but now that you've escaped let's start.

If you're a forgiving empath no matter what you endure. That was my Christian problem, for sure.

Once I learned what people were like/the need to separate God gave me a mansion with a locked gate.

I sinned by walking in muddy waters--being part of the noise/chaos of tolerance and open borders.

PEOPLE LOVERS OR VIRTUE SIGNALERS?

You say you love everyone but don't give me that bull it's just virtue-signaling for a loving image Missy.

People are such a waste of time. Alone you have all of history's men to know--it's called the Great Mind.

I'm through with you, now I'm gonna investigate ancestors and other Great Minds coming before.

How could anyone tolerate all this and not draw lines? That's not a people-lover, it's one of the blind.

I'm through thinking about details and just want sensual. Rain on a tin roof, the wind through the window.

Stop studying and let it percolate man. Let it seep in by comparisons/deep thinkin', you'll be winning.

He was eaten up by jealousy cuz he couldn't compare to me and lost his power/looks after discarding me.

Never go back and the embarrassment is over. Once repented of [no renege], it never happened.

SOUL MURDER

Make it and keep it ERASED: STAY AWAY.

Above all you must block the narcissist on all social media as well. All connections wiped out, do it now.

It was HIM who let the demons in who degraded me then, after which I took the blame for the whole thing.

Hey, if I never go back then you don't exist and it never happened cuz it's all been ERASED.

BE EXCLUSIVE, NOT INCLUSIVE

We're not to be inclusive but EXCLUSIVE. We're to draw lines, drop boundaries, screen out THEN live.

After working thru/getting over the narcissist's sting you won't want him again. Open to new friends.

Since the silent treatment is relational abuse you must go NO-CONTACT of course, not tighten then noose.

Cycle of abuse: idealize [adore/love bomb], devalue [insult, belittle], discard, hoover [make up].

Lockdown is a dress rehearsal for a global warming police state. It's not going away once it's our reality.

My self-partner side has determined you are not good enough to be with my inner child so BE GONE.

The left believes in "equality" but not liberty. We don't have freedom cuz the left is in charge, see?

With the goal of Equality they'll cut off your legs to fit their bed cuz liberty is never preferred instead.

The minute you go no-contact you'll start to remember things--will you ever! This guy was a bummer.

SILENT TREATMENT IS THE RUDDER

SOUL MURDER

Steal the spotlight from him and I'd get the silent treatment, affection-withholding unexplained.

You were too jovial or social: you get the silent treatment with no explanation, over/again here we go.

If you don't know about narcissistic abuse you're constantly looking inward: what did I do?

They use meanness/silence as a clutch to maintain power in the relationship--a giant endless irritant.

Up and down. all around: constant uncertainty, you're never truly free to be you're just UNHAPPY.

Narcissistic abuse is so common it oughta be required education, saving decades of frustration.

If the narc can make you jealous they get a little smirk on their face--they own you again in any case.

As you become more desperate you become his puppet, can't you see that? On a string: so tragic!

THROW HER A BONE

"Throw her a bone" the perpetrator says. Take note of this and never see him again, NOW be blessed.

He's a rotten apple/you must never see him again. You got so used to him/thought he was your friend.

To get him to stop ignoring her she'll admit to things she didn't even do--his control makes her crazy Sue.

To end his silence she'll give him sexual favors she wouldn't normally do, poor pathetic Sue.

She'll do ANYTHING to make the pain of the silent treatment STOP. This is relational rot!

SOUL MURDER

This dynamic gives the narc his supply. He's more in control than you, he's more worthy too!

Mature people with communication skills do NOT give the silent treatment which is cowardly, manipulative.

Of course he never stopped, he was rewarded every time. We either see the system or we're blind.

A highly exalted spirit is born into a family of addictions and crap. What a terrible shock, imagine that.

We're born into people who are wounded, our mind gets corrupted then decades later we MAY wake up.

THE INVADING NARCISSIST

Were you taught you had no right to personal boundaries? When they were busted did you get angry?

When they invaded me and I got angry I was ruthlessly punished for it--it was all MY fault, see?

As an empath I'm overwhelmed with information and data with people in the room, I must just be alone.

The invading narcissist would fill my house with his people and I'd go wild, not knowing why I was so riled.

My reality goes from peaceful hills with harvest to mad max chaos in a minute: that's the EMPATH.

I suppose I got a rep as an insane woman rather than pity for this invasion by the crazy social generation.

Even thinking about it riles me up. My nervous system memory flares up with pain at just the thought.

The reason I went crazy at the invasion by a buncha drunk teens was I didn't love people enough? Oh yah...

SOUL MURDER

Once going no-contact there's no going back. It's over so you can begin to heal: lay in the sun/take naps.

From thinking "why is she thinking that, I see what he's doing" to a calming breeze and beautiful view.

It's pretty hard to lay boundaries while in their midst, they'll object to it. Just fade out/stick to it.

He filled my house with people/my mind with confusion and I'm so bloody glad to be rid of him.

YOUR KID'S EVIL FRIENDS

Can you tell your kids you don't want their friends around without being called a hater/bigot and dumb?

Without defenses against it, I felt I was in a bubble constantly getting pierced by the rabble.

She doesn't draw lines--she includes everything and it's rather sickening. She's not of God, depressing.

She doesn't draw lines and that's called "loving". She can't see her descent into hell and treachery.

Your unique being can't rule your own mind--your reactions punishable by the conforming kind.

My reaction is to "leave, get out, go away, stay away and always call first", for serenity's my only thirst.

They said I was over-attached to animals but in truth I was under-attached to humans but still needed love.

It was a long road to ground myself, put boundaries up, honor my feelings: decades for my own reality.

ROAD BACK TO ME: BOUNDARIES

SOUL MURDER

The first part of the process was the road back to me but that HAD to come with boundaries [free to be].

You hurt me, that's it--now that it's over I'm really lit with fire, the enthusiasm and creativity of a prophet.

How wonderful: I'm a professional in total control gating out the rabble and not manipulated like years ago.

TROUBLES FROM ATTACHMENT TRAUMAS

There's enough existential loss and impermanence, I didn't need more from this.

Happiness or constant loss, grief and deep sadness that never resolves itself?

When I saw I didn't have to live in that grief realm I felt a breeze, the sun flowed in.

I didn't have to live confined or a product of my family history, I was free/me.

Freedom: You are no longer STUCK in that family system or any of the extended kin.

Goodbye to chronic grieving: feel the EXHAUSTION which kept you from living.

You're just realizing that being STUCK in this place is no longer working for you, so HERE GOES:

THE MESSAGE: YOU DON'T MATTER

Attachment trauma: you aren't heard nor seen making you more attached to the mean.

Its a PROFOUND experience of unmet relational needs: not being heard nor seen.

Born clear we mal-adapt to an INSANE world whether culture or other boys/girls.

SOUL MURDER

To feel wildly diminished by the experience of being disconfirmed like you don't exist.

It's a no-win dead-end dysfunctional exchange: attached = deranged.

Just one slight change--NO CONTACT--opens up new worlds of relief, delight, growth, genius.

It is just torture to the adult child's nervous system to go through this again.

They're half in/half out or not at all--so they have the leverage to hurt more.

YOU'RE NUMBER ONE OR NOT AT ALL!

The message is: You don't have any value and connecting with you has no value.

This is how this dynamic belittles a person's sense of self and it hurts like hell.

This dynamic cultivates shame, a feeling in tribes from not being connected/engaged.

The adult child cuts out the chronic source of pain, confusion and longing: a happy person again.

Reject this farce lest you feel shame and question worth like your early child or worse.

Just think of the hurt/pain of exclusion/diminishment knowing you'll never feel it again.

Things move on/the seasons change. Happy life is based on acceptance/learning new ways.

The deep injuries of attachment traumas in dysfunctional families cause disease.

CHILDREN OF DYSFUNCTION: CHRONIC LOSS

The children in the dysfunctional family will experience chronic loss, grief and sadness.

SOUL MURDER

You aren't worth it/don't matter enough to ever come to mind so that's tough.

You want relationship but they want none--tho' it's "family" cut attachment, son.
It's a terrible existence if your identity depends on it so cut it loose, you MUST.

Their indifference means the adult child is disempowered but only if still involved.

The recovered adult child stays INTACT by remembering these words: NO CONTACT.

The attempt to relate becomes a trauma trigger/attachment injury reminding him of a lifetime of the same.

Even hearing of them is a trigger for the unresolved lifelong attachment injury.

This dynamic belittles your sense of self and cultivates shame as a chronic no-win, ok?

DON'T REACTIVATE OLD WOUNDS

It's just that system that caused it but victims universalize it: he's the culprit.

Detach from THAT system and the whole world opens up cuz it was just THEM.

Every time it reactivates that wound and your history and you end in misery.

In a system the one least interested has the control--recurrent rejection gets old.

The person less invested has more control in the relationship? Man, think of that!

Just by not being interested they have the power if you want their participation.

It's crazy making and sets the adult child up for repeated, chronic trauma/relapse.

63

SOUL MURDER

It's chronic rejection ONLY if you want that relationship and that's quite an insight.

You are repeatedly denied emotional connection and yet invited to stay in.

Denied emotional connection with an expectation to accept the worthless relation.

What is missing is the adult child being seen, herd or understood--may as well be dead.

And so we accept what is: we gave it a go but there is no family, it was the past.

ACCEPTANCE REACHED BRINGS REVERSAL

Acceptance reached brings a reversal in one's life. ACCEPT IT, then joy is rife.

They had no interest in knowing you so move on, life is short, find more appropriate.

It's crazymaking cuz it links back to the painful history unresolved then we fall down.

The chronic but unacknowledged rejection undermines trust, safety and comfort.

It's a low level, subtle, compromised level of rejection made worse by its deception.

It's an ongoing, chronic, unsettled feeling of being stuck in limbo: let this go.

You are constantly denied the satisfaction of being fully received as a unique being.

You're still attempting to interact, engage and relate despite this old freight?

The adult child learns to avoid the familiar trauma triggers and attachment injuries.

Can you avoid the torturous attachment triggers occurring for a lifetime?

SOUL MURDER

The message is: You don't have any value nor does any meeting with you.

Living in a world defined by grief and loss where mom is saddened and disappointed.

Living in a world of loss, repeatedly orienting to frustration and disappointment.

Feel what the early and adult child had to endure: the constant tension thru the years.

CONSTANT PAIN BECOMES THE NORM

Because it is constant it becomes our norm, familiar means from the family.

I know this so well: I'm living in a world of grief and loss--the opposite of boss.

Instead of railing about these recognitions see it was your training before graduation.

The crazymaking world says: This is normal, we must endure, it's just the way it is.

After living in a world of chronic disappointment minimized as normal we've had it.

It's a framework of grief until I BECOME grief from chronic loss unresolved.

I saw the religious bloodline ended with me vs. two evil offshoots, and was free.

The reality of grief is created from attachment-trauma and I pray you see this.

I know it hurts that they didn't want to know you but your acceptance opens new.

So it's your own family, so what? The world is filled with fakes and the spiritually lost.

It's your desiring attachment and to be known that's causing the trouble so let it go.

SOUL MURDER

Not detaching completely is a chronic source of pain, confusion and longing. NO CONTACT, amen.

Keep saying: "It's just THEM not everyone, I overcame a crazymaking situation".

Facing shock that family didn't know you [yet others wanted to] opens you to new.

APATHY HAS THE POWER

If they have no interest but you want relationship they have the power, get it?

SAY: This will never happen to me: unbalance with me on the begging end.

The land bursts with new opportunities now that you're open having cut loose idiots.

She wanted to grandstand it, hot shot it, you know she was doing that.

Feminism is an elitist club only for a certain brand of woman with a liberal agenda.

Women don't know how to think and bring up non-issues: she politicians.

They treat male congressmen as they treat husbands: now we see an inversion.

Men are nice to faultfinding nags until they're not: congressmen are standing up.
Neighbors: I may hear their parties but never see em. Inward, solid, decent.

Here for an emergency but other than that no social expectations just discovery.

The true definition of feminism is thinking independently but that's prohibited.

SOMATIC NARCISSISM: CULTURE IN DECLINE

AOC is destructive, despicable and deceitful. Newt Gingrich

SOUL MURDER

Omar wants to degrade us into eating dogs then says we haters only love our dogs.

AOC calls them concentration camps: medical, two rooms, sports and three meals a day plus snacks.

Hate speech is whatever the left says it is in order to take your speech.

God darkens the heart of those who abandon Him then abandons the darkened heart.

The degenerate culture is all somatic narcissism. They don't care about the money just attention.

It's the result of childhood neglect: To get a rise outa you they'll do anything I expect.

You're judged by the reactions of others not yourself. This is social fascism and it's hell.

The dumb thug changes his view of you--instantly--when others do too.

The perceptions of the dumb thug fascist is totally socially-driven and he'll be killin'.

They NEVER see true reality but how the social sees it which changes every minute.

Living in this leftist-social matrix is the basis for insanity especially for the creative.

And it's the artistic-creative one in the system who is made the scapegoat: hmmm.

SOCIAL POLITIX

I pray you never get caught up in this system that almost killed me as the deviant one.

They don't enjoy the fabulous mansion just the jealousy which results I imagine.

SOUL MURDER

Plastic surgery isn't to enjoy beauty but the attention which results: social sluts.

It's all **ATTENTION**: that is the interaction, the opposite to the inner journey I'm lovin'.

By depending on reactions their ship is sunk for obvious reasons: the changing seasons.

Since it's based on reaction which gets desensitized so needs more, it gets really weird.

SICK SQUAD

Dangers of doing everything for attention and effect: it destroys the culture in fact.

But: True substance takes years like a fine wine or stew on simmer it's more than perfect.

If you're high no one will make friends cuz they don't wanna suck up but if you slip down they'll scapegoat.

AOC: You mean she **RULES** just cuz she's beautiful? Only in a nation of fools.

Ha Ha AOC and the gang make all dems look stupid even those with liberal ideas--this is fabulous.

Those freshmen women are no match for Trump but they think they are--how embarrassing blind stars.

GET RID OF EM! Arrogant female power drive is so embarrassing to behold.

When you cut a man's tongue out you don't prove him a liar only that you're afraid of what he has to say.

The squad can spew vile hateful things to the president then go crazy with accusation when he fights back.

Trump has now flushed out the democrats who huddle in fear around the squad, now they'll ALL be gone.

SOUL MURDER

Trump has now flushed out the democrats who huddle in fear around the squad, now they'll ALL be gone.

OMAR is uniquely off-putting as her superior patronizing attitude comes through/she's a hater too.

DAM DEMS DRUNK AND DISGUSTED

Speech must be banned for their truths to remain unchallenged nor any other hidden truths revealed.

DEMS shift the subject, ignore facts then use name-calling--thought you should know that to be ready.

Her strength is not thinking but conviction: that she puts her repugnant ideas out in a sincere way man.

Anxiety is like sitting in a rocking chair. You just sit there back and forth but never get anywhere.

Madam Currie did not need female role models to investigate radioactivity, just a passion to understand, ok?

WHEN GOD GIVES YOU UP

When God abandons a society it becomes pornographic first then the curse.

God gives em over to degrading passions--second thing happening to the falling nation.

It's just sexual lust uncontained not a group with rights like they're all sayin'.

They don't need us to become advocates they just need us not to care.

Not ok: It is nothing more than a sexual lust which is unnatural, twisted and uncontained.

Meekness is strength and power under control.

Instead of inter-relating it's now two computer stations in a household and little else.

SOUL MURDER

We're dealing with people who hate our country and it's been that way since the sixties.

They DON'T love America if they want open borders which means crime, drugs, trafficking.

Democrats have become the party of Open Borders and bringing in the hordes.

They use the word "racism" to win any debate and it has cheapened the term.

Identity politics-driven, victim-centric, orange man bad: this is regressive leftism.

THE TIDES ARE TURNING

All of NYC went dark when they arrested the Clintons so there'd be no escapin'

You've made your decision: never listen to em.

That's just how it goes and everyone knows it.

Look around: people are obese--they don't need to eat thrice.

The main characteristic of the Jezebel Spirit is taking over when given the chance.

When everyone's a racist, no one's a racist.

With the left any dumb trend that comes along is immediately accepted by the throng.

Heal from attachment trauma with self reparenting--this is recovery thru the creative.

White privilege: feeling guilty over something you have no control over--how racist.

It's not your season until season's change. Like it was hot but now it's not so prepare for the stage.

There's no white privilege on the basketball court. Jessie Watters

SOUL MURDER

It's not that you're old or not old, in an ageist society it's the fact that they'd say it: it's cold.

We wanna be with our own. One kind of God's wrath is being suddenly surrounded by strangers.

You're happy in your home then 100 strangers invade your house--wouldn't you want em out?

Because it doesn't affect them directly they couldn't care less. But wait, it's coming for you sis.

ALL DISPARITIES BLAMED ON RACISM {it gets old}

All disparities are blamed on racism despite having a black president twice ma'am.

It was a weaselly inference not a valid question so get outa my face madame.

Say no and don't argue about it. Don't let him tell you it happened once so now it's a contract.

Events happen we just can't get over. These traumas of attachment are torture.

Things happen, life changes--how will you adapt, that's the barometer of your wellness.

Conservatives, Christian and whites are nice until they're not, then watch out.

I have a husband, two dogs and two cats and everyone's as happy as it gets.

MacCarthyism: Fascistic doctrine that associating with someone is same as sharing their views.

We're nice until we're not. We're not gonna take it anymore so libtard snowflakes watch out!

When everything they say is self-discrediting enjoy your victory celebration every day.

SOUL MURDER

Crazy comparisons diminishing historical catastrophes saying it's the same as you and me.

Without God in their heart they're given over to great delusion: Democrats make no sense hon'

AMERICAN VALUES MAY BE GONE FOREVER

Are you upset that American values will be gone forever if they win, you traitors?

People have bad days, they should be able to make mistakes. But this, are you kidding mate?

AOC's an intellectual coward: throwing out that stuff but refusing to debate it ever.

In this era calling someone a dumb bigot racist ends the relationship immediately, even family.

Omar comes from an elite tribe of Somalis whose specialty is slavery to this day.

You don't go to Mexico and run your mouth how it sux--they'd say get the hell out.

The household should run like a swiss watch on everything from wash to removing trash.

You know what's going on now, no more need be said--now concentrate on repairing instead.

They're hit all at once and come from a place of unskilled aggression, embarrassin'

People are mean as hell and I have boundaries--don't want leaks from all the treachery.

If it continues we're still viewing the world thru the lens of the younger (rejected) self.

SOUL MURDER

SOMETHING WRONG WITH ME

"Must be something wrong with me" cuz they didn't want to see, engage with or know you.

"I must be unlovable, I don't deserve love, must be something wrong with me". misfit song

In modern culture we're living in a very immature psychology--not truly wizened really.

The narcissistic wound to the self blocks normal development to the adult.

They were either too dumb or distracted to know you or even want to, so you lost YOU.

Especially women view themselves thru the eyes of others: how the torturous system smothers.

FELT SICK AS "HELL"

Felt sick as hell going and then how you were actin' but now it's ok cuz we're home again.

Not only are they dumb the fakers see your great aspirations as delusions of grandeur.

Childish undisciplined aggression, like adultery or getting back some other way hon'.

One response to not being noticed is to become the best in everything, for a response.

The other response to not being known is to implode into the self and disappear (low down).

In this world it's not safe to be you so you hide or stay distant making no commitments.

The misfit feels shame {not good enough] so must build a persona but it's always lame.

SOUL MURDER

Not only was it not safe to be me, people wouldn't let me be me so I had to write out this theory.

I saw in a small desert town how all perceptions were socially-driven and it was crazy-makin'.

The process of becoming is hijacked by the system's narcissistic wound to the identity.

They never sought to know me nor know me now so grief took over 'til growth from above.

RESPONSE TO APATHY IS PRIMAL RAGE

The response to not being known then and now: primal RAGE at this existential cage.

Description of the old system: continuously tapping into a river of grief and shame.

Well after decades of it the crushing grief finally broke it all open. I was free, nature moves on.

People in my family just didn't want to know me even today and that brought rage/shame.

The profound ignoring, the profound rejection which goes on then one day we say "IT'S OVER".

When I discover their apathy it brings personal rage linking to a primal rage then shame.

I ended up in the back of a dusty ghost town facing utter abandonment/pure isolation.

People do anything to avoid feelings of isolation and abandonment, so they adapt/I didn't.

In a small dusty cabin I found myself and the quintessential and I was in bliss ya' know.

SOUL MURDER

I realized I didn't have to orient to grief anymore, as I had my entire life before.

With grief we become hyper-aroused with details: the hypervigilant, aroused mind.

NIP IT IN THE BUD OR PANIC ATTACKS?

Instead of nipping in the bud/declaring independence you have panic attacks instead.

It works subconsciously: You're in a system of self's vulnerability on the brink of tragedy.

The current relationship is a stand-in for the childhood grief of the one never realized.

Childhood longing for relationship that never happened leaks out thru crying over the current stand-in.

Attachment injuries coded from unresolved trauma leaks thru current drama.

The abandonment trauma is easily triggered as free-floating unresolved energy.
It's a "leak" when the present circumstance reminds you of that past creep.

It is hell staying in the place of NON-CLOSURE. It can go on for decades, for sure.

Non-closure suffering invites chaos. Activates nervous system with flood of possibilities then devastation.

THE WOUNDED CHILD IS STILL CRYING

Getting back to my favorite subject of how I was ignored as a child and went wild.

The wounded child is still crying. When you feel it welling up you may quickly start doing something.

Through all that trouble I learned what I didn't want and that should mean worlds to us, huh?

SOUL MURDER

What I wanted was solitude, my own thing, no interruptions, my own reality totally.

Connection--involvement--means TROUBLE so the misfit's entire structure becomes a bubble.

I remember major turning points downward as my identity was wounded.

Major points when thinking I was someone I became suddenly no-one and was shunned.

If your personna's based on fake to compensate for the wound at the gate: APATHY.

THEY'LL CRAWL BACK WHEN MONEY

Sure they're gonna come back when there's money but what about way back then honey

Angry threats, bitter resentful words, ugly demands--when have you had enough man.

The message is: Don't feel the bad feelings, let's just try to be good.

A SURVIVAL mechanism says: I can't feel that.

We are people who are frightened of our own reflection, our own feeling state.

Not belonging: To live life day after day feeling invisible, disconnected, abandoned, rejected, neglected.

The narcissistic wound: not known, not seen, not heard, not valued--it takes its toll.

Sunglasses denotes you're different from them and they're not getting in.

To protect the emotions the attachment style or personality structure is designed to stay disconnected.

Other tactics: Don't warehouse stuff (lay up) and don't manufacture it (cuz you're on a roll): relax, pull back.

SOUL MURDER

Another strategy of the disconnected is to reverse matrices and compensate by being "NICE".

NICE FAÇADE: COMFORTING BUT DEVASTATING

The NICE presentation is comforting at first but then drives others crazy as a deceitful curse.

It's all a system: The Misfits' personality structures were designed to avoid connection.

When alone in my desert paradise I thrived but when I got involved it was misery day and night.

In civil society it's good to be nice it makes us relax but in systems it's leverage with a high tax.

The nice one [tho' a menace] is accepted but the scapegoat explodes so he's the culprit.

The nice lady is more likely to forgive without repentance or justify sin in personal friends.

I have no fake personna, I'm defined by my work, my work ethic and my love of America.

It may be a lonely life but not really when your creativity is rife and you gotta be ready.

I'm finally complete/everything's locked into place and I'm set, flying high mentally/aced.

THIS is the day the Lord hath made and I'm done, complete, locked and loaded.

Get that: Their apathy caused a wound in your identity compensated by a fake personna.

The amount of self-righteous anger and snotty social climbing was evident with you honey.

SOUL MURDER

Deep-seated anger: blowing up all the time over petty stuff while ignoring real danger.

THE FALLEN HERO SYNDROME

I went from an echo-chamber of adoring sycophants to a dungeon of liberal feminists.

Once you're on the downward spiral it's impossible to stop, it's scary being caught up.

I went from temporary stardom back to original system and wow what a shock in comparison.

The shock was the ontologically fatal insight: my world was not what I thought it to be.

What should I submit to their "review"? Who are they--I'd never bow before man that way.

It's the Fallen Hero Syndrome when previous fans become foes as you're goin' down.

It was so horrible as the Jezebel Spirits took control because women hate women ya' know.

You were free as a child then suddenly have to conform in a narrow groove of abuse and ridicule.

BE LIKE TRUMP: THE SHREWD, SNEAKY SAVANT

Everybody's a psychologist and to them everyone's a narcissist so ignore em all and persist.

You were an optimistic and talented dreamer called "crazy with definite delusions of grandeur".

The fallen hero going down is controlled by a demon spirit and must get out somehow.

SOUL MURDER

Then I was forced to abort my mission on the brink of a breakthrough: that won't happen now too.

It's gonna get done in spite of you so why not relax and take leisure as it comes through.

Confronting conversion therapy: calling it "normal" not helping people to overcome it.

They are violent vile predators: recruiters not reproducers.

LEAKS FROM EARLY TRAUMA

It wasn't your rejection that brought relapse but the leak from EARLY traumatic events.

It wasn't your boring lackluster self triggering this panic but how it reminds me of my titanic.

It wasn't you triggering downfall of a great person but the leak of years of tears like an ocean.

Never take success or good breaks for granted cuz you can lose it all [AGAIN] in a minute.

Password to God: thankfulness, and realizing that what He giveth He can taketh away.

SYSTEM INVERSIONS AND CYCLES

You went from a bright happy light to a black cloud of tyranny under illogic, a blight.

When you were up but now down they'll beat you as clown, who did you think you were before now?

The more high you were before, the worse life will be now--that's system inversion ya' know.

You rattled their cage with envy before, all that stored bad energy will now target you sir.

SOUL MURDER

Tho' it seems the hero is doing nothing he's actually doing something very important for mankind.

Those were the silent years--appearing as ZERO but actually an inward journey to miracles.

While I appeared to be doing nothing it was so rich I ended the journey writing 100 books.

Therapy: See what people are really like. Visit a concentration camp or fail in their eyes.

To witness the depths of human depravity as its victim it's very hard to get up again.

ANOREXIA PSYCHOSA AND ATTACHMENT TRAUMAS

This victimization by previous fans miscombines with sins used as coping mechanisms.

Only the strongest/most godly can pull themselves back up and resume being on top.

By far the greatest tendency is for the hero to continue his descent and get sick or die.

If an early trauma has occurred without adaptive tools the crisis reverts back to survival: food.

Having been ignored/disconfirmed in the system the heavy spirit reverts to basics, not friends.

Anorexia is an emotional illness and builmia is a desperate coping mechanism I tell ya.

An early trauma (event) occurs without tools to handle it so links to biological: food or sex.

Massive nutritional intake distracts then purgation temporarily keeps her on top.

SOUL MURDER

She doesn't know why it works this temporary remedy of demons, that is possession.

No tools to handle trauma so calls out for mama symbolized by food: manna.

Everyone hated her for this subconscious mania holding her together in spite of ya.

They used to call it consumption--man's appetites and the acquisitive spirit (to acquire it).

The overcompensating perfectionist female who hasn't self-realized will never admit it's emotional.

FOOD MEANS MOTHER

Food means mother. Uncompleted mourning from lost affections and survival needs triggered.

Triangulation Trigger: two against one--never knows what hit her 'til seeing the system.

Present relational traumas trigger the original bomb and survival panic sets in.

An angry, drunk, irrational mother means murder to infant--developmentally she's stuck.

What could be a more basic clinger than food to an infant, for sex hasn't entered the picture yet.

Since it is a survival surrogate it is clung to much more tenaciously and resistant to therapy.

Sexual addictions are later developmentally so are not as obdurate in this *survival category*.

It's not a desire to be skinny except insofar as it's survival-based to avoid obesity.

GLYCATION WAS MY CRITERION

SOUL MURDER

DISCOVERY takes a trivial fact and brings it forward as the whole matrix as the bottom becomes the top.

That paradigmatic flip-flop in science is GLYCATION: Fat causes it not sugar and it's the key to aging.

Not all carnivores show glycation so they trot those out to the nations but it eventually quickens aging.

He looked great at first on the carnivore diet but compare his pictures, you'll see it turned on him a lot.

Not all meat eaters show glycation so they trot those out. They're pandering to a spirit I want nothing of.

OLD LADY VEGAN DIET

Being a fastarian is not being anorexic so shut up with that. One is healthy the other's not: fact.

I don't get angry like some vegans do, that solves nothing. Especially as lowcarb explodes in popularity.

There are meat-eaters and there are meat-abstainers and that's just the way it is, no judgement from us.

Old Lady Diet: Breakfast is smoothie made with fruit, lunch is delicious salad, a starch then skipping dinner too.

MANUAL FOR SUPERIOR MEN: A NEW SOCIAL PSYCH

If God sees you complaining about what He's rescued you from it's ingratitude so stop it chum.

100 KAREN KELLOCK BOOKS

AFFINITY OR MISERY
AGELESS CORNUCOPIA
AMERICA AWAKE!
AMERICA'S DAFT ERA
ARTS OF PALEO FASTING
AUTOPHAGY ON CHEATERS
BACKSTABBING NEUROTICS
BETRAYAL TRAUMA
BOOMERS AND BROKENNESS
BOOT ON NECK
CHAMPION GUIDES
COMMIE NUTHOUSE
COMMIES
COMMUNIST SPIRIT
CONTAGION OF MADNESS
CONTAGIOUS MADNESS
CULTURE CLASH BASHED
DAFT LEFT
DAILY FASTARIAN
DAM RATS
DIVERSITY IS CRUELTY
E-RACE WHITE
EVIL FREAKS (Beyond Gross)
THE END OR A BEND?
FEMALE BULLIES AND FEMI-NAZIS
FEMALE CARNALITY
FEMALE DUMB DOWN
FEMALE POWER DRIVE
FEMINISM AND RUIN 1 & 2
FIX FOR MISFITS
FOOLS & TRAMPS
FREEDOM SPEAKING
FRENEMY ENABLER
FRENEMY LIAR
FRENEMY THIEF
FRENEMY TRAITOR
TRENEMY TYRANT
GENIUS IS HELD DOWN
GLOBALISLAM
GOD USES THE FLAWED
HAZE OF THE LATTER DAYS

THE HERD IN WORDS
HIX POLITIX
HOW THEY RUINED US
JUST SKIP DINNER
LE FEMME AND THE COMMUNIST SPIRIT
LIBERAL CHAOS & ROT
LIBERAL DOUBLETHINK
LIBERAL GALL 1 & 2
LIBERAL SHOVE-DOWNS
LOCK YOUR GATE
LOSERS and Femme Fatales
MANUAL FOR SUPERIOR MEN
MODERN ART FROM HELL
MOSTLY FAKE
NOTES TO CHAMPS 1 & 2
OVERCOME FRENEMIES
PC MAKES US CRAZY
PEOPLE ARE CRUEL
PEOPLE PROBLEMS 1 & 2
PERSECUTED GENIUIS
POLI-PSYCH MYSTERIES
PRETENTIOUS SLOBS
QUEEN BEE
RED NEW DEAL
RETURNING TO FIRST NATURE
SEASON OF TREASON
SEPARATE MEANS HOLY
SOCIAL HYPNOTISM
SOLITUDE SOLUTION
SUPERCILIOUS
THE SCHOOLS SCREWED EM UP
TOAD TO PRINCE
TRIALS CYCLES
TRUMP VS. GROUP
TRUST IN TRASH
THE TRUTH ABOUT PEOPLE
UNDERHEANDEDLY CLEVER
WALK TALL WITHIN WALLS
WE'RE NOT ALL ONE
WINNERS SKIP DINNER
WORK OR SMERK

AUTHOR BIO

Karen Kellock Ph.D.

Ph.D Political Psychology, UCI 1976
Post-Doctoral: UCI Medical School
Department of Psychiatry
Grants NIMH, NIAAA

Ph.D. dissertation "A Systems-Theoretic View of Pathologic Interaction" made an early mark as the "Wife of the Alcoholic Syndrome". Postdoctoral research at UCI Medical, Dept. of Psychiatry on the systems surrounding pathology on NIMH and NIAAA federal grants: *The Contagion of Madness: The Psychology of Neurotic Interaction and Pathological Systems*. Therapy tool Therapeutic Playwriting introduced the play *Mary and Murv: Gruesome Twosomes in the Alcoholic Marriage*. She taught Abnormal Psychology and Pathological Systems Theory at UC and CSU campuses and developed "the Debris Theory of Disease" in five books and website: (www.karenkellock.org): *Champion Guides, Daily Fastarian, Just Skip Dinner, Arts of Paleo Fasting, Ageless Cornucopia. Manual for Superior Men is a* pick-it-up-anywhere book that you can't put down (20,000 Kellockialisms) and ever on your desktop it should be found (or this Ebook for superior wordsearch of new jargon).